A Christian Voice in Education: Distinctiveness in Church Schools

A Christian Voice in Education:

Distinctiveness in Church Schools

George Carey
David Hope
John Hall

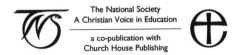

The National Society
A Christian Voice in Education

a co-publication with
Church House Publishing

National Society/Church House Publishing
Church House
Great Smith Street
London SW1P 3NZ

ISBN 0 901819 63 8

First published 1998 by The National Society and Church House
Publishing

Printed by The Cromwell Press Ltd, Trowbridge, Wiltshire

Contents

Introduction

Church schools themselves embody the truth that a
context of firm principle suffused by faith and love is the
best and right basis for learning and growing.

The Archbishop of Canterbury

One criticism of Church schools in recent years has been their
lack of conviction. The inspection process over the last five years
has revealed this to be a fallacy. Of course some schools could
make a more positive attempt to define their Christian character
more clearly but, in the main, the words of the Archbishop of
Canterbury quoted above can be fully justified.

Church schools should be distinctive because at their heart lies a
confidence in the love of God and God's love for his creation. The
Church school where it is safe to speak of God and of his love is
a 'safe' school, a school where faith and commitment can be
expressed, only without fear. Church schools are, in one sense,
guardians of the faith, not coercive or aggressive; rather they
represent the interface of the Church and society. Some of our
schools have children from many different faiths and none and it
is entirely appropriate that the Church through the warmth and
receptivity of its schools is able to welcome those children. It is
the warmth of hospitality and care; it is not the hard face of
proselytism. Our schools should be places where religious belief,
worship and the love of God are found in relationships, between
pupils, between staff and between the Church and the school.
They are, therefore, guardians of the faith, a light to follow as the
next millennium begins.

In 1997, the Anglican secondary schools completed the first cycle
of inspection and, before moving on to the next six-year cycle, the

end of the era was marked with a conference in York. The conference was addressed by the Archbishop of York and Barbara Wintersgill HMI. The Archbishop's speech is included in full.

Dr Hope focuses on two words – quality and excellence, and develops the theme that in addition to these qualities the school is a community of persons; it is the person that is prior to the institution. Schools have to be concerned that structures and frameworks do not inhibit the quality and excellence in relationships between staff and pupils. He recalls Archbishop Temple's insistence on the word 'spiritual' being used in the 1944 Education Act rather than 'religious', in order to indicate a broader and more tolerant tone – a deliberate attempt to be inclusive rather than exclusive.

The following year, 1998, representatives of head teachers of Anglican primary schools, (for they also had reached the end of the first cycle of inspections) gathered at Church House in Westminster to hear the Archbishop of Canterbury and Her Majesty's Chief Inspector of Schools, Mr Chris Woodhead. The Archbishop of Canterbury's speech is also included in full in this book.

'Christianity in action, at the service of our fellow human beings and excellent education which flows from Christian beliefs' was the message of Dr Carey. Church schools are important to the Church for they are places where the incarnation continues; they are places where children learn the story of the Christian faith and can grow in Christian discipleship. Controversially, the Archbishop states that schools can provide a context in which the children can experience the language and attitude of worship. Church schools, he concludes, are distinctive in being explicit Christian communities that unashamedly offer a Christian vision to guide our young.

Chris Woodhead did not address the specific issue of Church schools but reflected on some general aspects arising from the experience of inspection. Among the points raised were:

1   a general improvement in teaching reflected in inspection judgements and the National Curriculum tests;

2   high expectation of pupils being essential;

3   *how* teachers teach is important;

4   schools should take responsibility for their own performance;

5   experience shows the only people who can make a difference to standards are head teachers;

6   if there is a weakness, it is the inability of some head teachers to have a finger on the quality of teaching in their school;

7   there is no need for schools to revamp all policies in their school before each inspection;

8   there must be better feedback, and the language of the reports more accessible to parents.

The conferences were designed as occasions when the value of Church schools could be recognized and endorsed while still acknowledging there is much to be achieved.

Canon John Hall, General Secretary of the National Society and the Board of Education of the Church of England adds his own reflections on the place of Church schools in the education provision of the twenty-first century. He draws attention to the opportunities the Church has through its 5,000 schools to offer an attractive account of the Christian faith and life to almost a million young people. During the twentieth century, the Church has not been consistent in valuing its schools nor has there been an agreed basis for development. He argues for more coherent planning for the future on the foundation of the present popularity and success of many Church schools.

Church of England schools have received a tremendous endorsement from the two Archbishops and, under the guidance and direction of John Hall, can look forward to the next century with confidence.

Alan S Brown

Director of the National Society's London RE Centre and the Church of England's RE Officer

The importance of Church schools

Archbishop of Canterbury, Dr George Carey

Church schools pose an uncomfortable challenge to all those who think of religion and ordinary life as two separate spheres. The more zealous enthusiasts for a gathered Church of holy people, separate from the wicked world outside, will be suspicious of our 4,500 Church of England primary schools as a pillar of the country's whole education system. They might be particularly suspicious of those schools' successful integration within the life of the school of so many pupils from families which subscribe to no organized religion or to another faith. Can these be Christian schools? What sort of 'Christianity' is that?

Most Church schools are even more of a headache for secular theorists and apostles of privatized belief and morals. It is bad enough for them that more than one in six primary pupils go to a Church of England Church school; it is much worse that they are on average so successful on educational criteria and so popular with parents. While some theorists of 'pluralism' would consign denominational schools to a past era, lo and behold here are thousands and thousands of families who do not go to church queuing up to send their children to Church schools, and here are Church schools doing on average very well in the examination league tables. What on earth is going on here?

My answer is: Christianity in action, at the service of our fellow human beings and excellent education which flows from Christian beliefs. And, last but not least, a lot of hard work by Church school head teachers, staff and governors, many of whom are here today! That is why it is such a delight for me to have this

1

opportunity to pay tribute to your tremendous contribution to Church and nation and to discuss some contemporary challenges and opportunities. Indeed, one of the most enjoyable aspects of my work as Archbishop is my many visits to schools every year. I am impressed by the dedication of so many teachers, in all our schools not only Church schools, and I value their immense contribution to our nation.

The first four-year round of OFSTED inspections of primary schools is virtually completed. Although the process is never comfortable, and can sometimes even be painful, I hope most of you will have been left with the satisfaction of a job well done as well as determination to make the most of the future.

Last year I was delighted to be able to write a letter in the National Society's Newsletter which goes to all Church schools congratulating many of the primary schools on featuring so well in the league tables. I also noted, however, that schools placed lower down were often doing excellent work in difficult circumstances and were being effective in 'adding value'. It is very appropriate that I should be able to re-iterate those comments here before so many of you who have contributed so much to the progress of your pupils. I hope we will be able to maintain and improve on this in the years to come. It represents a tremendous effort on the part of our primary schools and says much about their high educational expectations as well as their strong Church school ethos.

So no doubt OFSTED have unearthed a lot of good news about your schools – our schools. Not only about the sort of success that shows up in league tables, but about the ethos, the coherent value base, the uninhibited attention to spiritual and moral as well as other dimensions of education. Thank God for that. However hard we all need to keep working for improvement, there is something worth celebrating.

I now want to dig deeper into the character and significance of Church schools – first in the life of the Church; and secondly in the wider society as it faces a new millennium.

The importance of schools

First, what is the importance of your schools to the Church? Church schools are so important, precisely because they are not perceived as separate, holy places dedicated to some separate realm called religion. They are in the thick of society, places where so many people are educated. Even more than most Church social projects, they make the link between faith and the aspirations of people – not in particular the sick, the elderly, the bereaved, the vulnerable or some other special category of need, but *all* kinds of children growing up. Christianity is seen not as a set of abstract doctrines, but as faith in a God of love acted out in the detail of school life.

It is not just for Christian people: most Church of England schools are open to many pupils who are not from Christian families. They are places where religion is de-mystified and where children can become not more pious, but more fully human. They are places where the incarnation continues, where the divine comes down to earth, where the Word is a living word which touches the lives of God's children and the communities in which they live. In short, Church of England schools earth the Church in broad sectors of the population keeping her looking outwards, in service to society at large, making constant links between faith and human need.

And Church schools have a licence, as it were, from their special Christian foundations, to attend wholeheartedly to the spiritual and moral dimensions of education. It is vital that many practising Christian families can send their children to Church schools in the confident expectation of an effective and coherent partnership

3

between family, school and parish church. You serve the Christian family as well as the wider community.

There was a time when it was difficult to detect the difference between many Anglican Church schools and County schools. It is not a criticism of County schools when I say that I am delighted that this is not so common these days. I do not mean that County schools are less good, but Church of England schools by their very nature are committed to maintaining a distinctive ethos which, fully in keeping with striving for the highest standards of education, should be explicitly Christian and Anglican. We owe it to our children to keep faith with this goal.

In an age where Sunday Schools have so markedly declined, your schools are the places where hundreds of thousands of children learn the story of Christian faith, grow in Christian discipleship and, through the example of Christian teachers and the experience of a Christian-based community, accept into their hearts and minds some real knowledge of the great truths which our Lord came to dramatize and teach. You have no need to be apologetic in integrating religious education and worship into the rounded formation of your pupils. You need not be inhibited in preparing them for the love and service of their neighbours. You can be bold and open in helping them begin to explore the great questions of life's meaning, death, faith, and the world beyond the surface of things. You are, and need to be, the trailblazers in these aspects of education, which flow naturally from your Christian foundations.

A good example of this is the National Society's current project on the Spiritual Development of Children from five to eleven years old. It is in collaboration with both Church and non-Church schools. It is exploring the most effective ways of ensuring that children's spiritual development is enhanced across the curriculum. It is just the sort of initiative the Church should be carrying out, drawing heavily on Church schools themselves. And another good example is the report and resource pack on

'Values in Church Schools', written by the head of a Church school and to be launched here later today. This should help us all as we continue to engage with the vital issue as to what values make our Church schools distinctive, and how we can best reflect them in all our work.

The development of a fully human being – measuring up to the stature of Christ – is not the task of the school alone. But schools have a major contribution to make. Children must learn to face questions of the meaning of life and death and the purpose of their own lives. They need to develop a sense of themselves as significant, unique and precious individuals, with the courage and confidence that flow from that realization.

There are opportunities for this spiritual development in every subject of the curriculum. But the best opportunity in the school is created by the act of worship, a time for reflection and prayer, a time to learn from the experiences and attitudes of men and women of faith, a time for every member of the school community to find space for themselves and for God.

Schools cannot require children to worship but they can and should create a context day by day in which children can experience the language and attitude of worship, can learn to worship and so learn their own infinite worth. There is plenty of good practice around and I hope schools, particularly Church schools, will continue to share good ideas in making this daily requirement a really rich contribution to school life.

I emphasize that the job of Church schools is not to try to get as many kids in the bag for the Church as possible. They do not serve that kind of narrow institutional purpose, and I know that you as educators would not put up with that. On the contrary, the starting point is the sharing of God's love, and the Christian values which flow from it, and hence the guiding principle is care and respect for the uniqueness and preciousness of every single child in your charge That is incompatible with being a forcing house. Yet no educational framework, whatever it claims, is neutral or value free. Church of England schools are explicit about their Christian value base and ethos as a rich, secure setting in which children can learn, grow and equip themselves for life.

Hence, our schools are a very large and fundamentally important dimension of the Church of England's mission and service to the nation. The whole Church needs to honour it, own it and support it in practical ways. I think we can be justly proud of the immense contribution Church schools have made to our nation. We were educating children long before a national education system was devised and we are part of it now.

The importance of Church schools for the wider society

I now turn to *the significance of Church of England schools for the wider society*. In a nutshell, it is becoming obvious to an ever larger number of people that a society without rules, without a strong sense of mutual responsibilities, love of neighbour and service to others is headed for disaster. It is also obvious to many of us that people who are affluent in material things will often lead impoverished lives if they are not nourished spiritually; if faith, hope and love are swamped by empty consumerism. I suggest that Church schools are in the front line when it comes to holding the line and then counter attacking.

I was very struck by Professor Michael Barber's thoughtful and widely publicized address to the Secondary Heads' Association in March about 'The Ethics of Education Reform'. It was interesting to observe someone other than an Archbishop being treated to such hysterical and tendentious criticisms. But the core of Professor Barber's message was this (and I quote):

The vigour and urgency with which we are seeking to modernize our education system is driven in part by the need to compete in a global market but at least as much surely by moral outrage at the rootlessness of so much modern life and by a belief that, together, we can and must do better if the generation currently in our schools is to find fulfilment.

I am delighted to hear the Head of the Government's Standards and Effectiveness Unit define his purposes in such terms. I am delighted that he insists that ethical education is a fundamental precondition of the good society, and that social cohesion requires a strong base of shared values and a rolling back of the tide of cultural relativism and what he calls 'rampant materialism'. As they say, 'I couldn't have put it better myself.' In fact, I have put it myself, many times, but then I am not the Head of Standards and Effectiveness!

In praising and associating myself with the central thrust of Professor Barber's address, I would like to suggest that in acting upon it and making a reality of it he needs all the allies he can get in the great Churches and other religious traditions of this country, not least in Church schools and colleges. Some of Professor Barber's phrases may have given the unintended impression of being dismissive of religion in general and Christianity in particular as a continuing source of moral and ethical enlightenment. Phrases such as 'in the absence of God and Marx, what are we to do?' seem to imply that God is dead, whereas over 70 per cent of people say they believe in God and 50 per cent say they pray regularly. In advancing his own arguments for an ethical underpinning of life, Professor Barber rather goes to town on the Australian philosopher Peter Singer, plus such luminaries as Fukuyama, Etzioni, Professor John Gray and even the Demos think tank. Not one contributor from a religious background – and there are plenty – gets a look in, nor the entire tradition of moral and ethical reflection nurtured by religious faith. No doubt that is because Professor Barber took for granted that religions have a firm ethical framework, he wanted to address people who subscribe to no religion. Perhaps this obscured the essentially positive character of Professor Barber's message.

I also found it strange that there is no reference in Professor Barber's address to the work of the School Curriculum and Assessment Authority (SCAA) and now the Qualifications and Curriculum Authority(QCA). It seems odd that a senior Government adviser, seeking to promote the importance of ethics in education, should appear to ignore the vital SCAA initiative on values in education, with its discovery of the strong shared values held across a wide cross section of society. Those are now enshrined in Government guidance which empowers and encourages schools to transmit the shared moral values of society to children as a deliberate aspect of their education. To my mind, the reality of shared values, now named and encouraged officially in the education system, is an even more significant building block than, for example, the philosophical insights of Peter Singer. Moreover, the SCAA and QCA initiatives have the advantage that they feed on religious insights among others; that representatives of religious traditions are active participants, contributors and friends. And that is how it needs to be if the tides of rampant materialism, moral relativism and social exclusion are to be turned.

It bears repeating that I concur wholeheartedly with Professor Barber's main concerns and I trust he will see Church schools as ready and willing partners in the task of contributing to the moral vision to which he is so clearly committed.

I come back to the contemporary debate about the purposes of education. There is much to encourage us, not least the overall thrust of Professor Barber's address. I am encouraged by the underlying concerns of the Professor Crick's Advisory Group

Report on citizenship education, and indeed I am pleased that the Secretary of State decided it was a priority to set up such a group. I warm to the Advisory Group's definition of citizenship education as three interrelated factors: social and moral responsibility, community involvement and political literacy. I appreciate their recognition that 'guidance on moral values and personal development are essential preconditions of citizenship'.

The Group also makes good points about the need to express moral values in civic and political as well as individual and family life: all very Church of England, if I may say so! I must, as an Archbishop, leave to others the debate as to the best means through which to ensure that those vital aspects of education are taken really seriously, and how the Crick Group's work can avoid running into the sands of negative or complacent reactions.

More generally, it is good that, at least at the level of rhetoric and sentiment, there is so much recognition that, while we need reform and adaptability in so many dimensions of life, the precondition of embracing such change successfully is a sturdy structure of values, a rootedness in the great spiritual and moral truths which do not change. Idolatry of what is new, simply because it is new, is the road to moral, social and ecological disaster. Modernization has its limits, and the limits relate to the accumulated wisdom of successive generations about the nature of human beings, human well-being and the good life.

That is where Church schools come in. They are as concerned as any other school to equip pupils for lives marked by rapid change, global competition and insecurity. But Church schools know in their viscera that this is not just about acquiring skills and good examination results. It is about forming people who have the moral strength and spiritual depth to hold to a course and weather ups and downs. It is about forming people who know that economic competition is not more important than family life and love of neighbour, and that technical innovation is not more important than reverence for the beauty of creation. It is about forming people who, however academically and technically skilful, are not reduced to inarticulate embarrassment by the great questions of life and death, meaning and truth. Church schools themselves embody the truth that a context of firm principles suffused by faith and love is the best and right basis for learning and growing.

Professor Barber was so right to express his concern that in a rootless and confused age with so many tugs on the time and attention of children, it is all too easy for them to lose their moral bearings. Schools, all schools, are moral communities which, through many different ways, nurture children on their way to adulthood and participation in society. Church schools are distinctive in being explicit Christian moral communities which unashamedly offer a Christian vision to guide our young.

Yes, we have a great past. And yes, we are part of the future, a part which both Church and wider society badly need. In two years we shall celebrate the second millennium of the birth of Jesus Christ. This faith has shaped our nation and continues through the work of churches and schools to shape the moral and spiritual vision of many of our citizens. In this task the Church schools play a vital role. While we must of course be respectful of those who do not wish explicit affirmations of faith expressed in our schools, let us not be apologetic nor reticent about beliefs and ideals which have made us what we are. Indeed, I am quite clear that our children need it, parents are requesting it and, I believe, our educational system and our country value it.

A Christian vision in education

Archbishop of York, Dr David Hope

I hope you will forgive my beginning this address to you all this morning with a text. I realize that I am not delivering a sermon nor are you here to be preached at! However, bearing in mind the theme for today, 'a Christian vision in education', I should like to set before you the words of St Paul from his Letter to the Philippians, chapter 4 verse 8: 'Finally, whatever is true, whatever is honourable, whatever is just, whatever is pure, whatever is lovely, whatever is gracious, if there is any excellence, if there is anything worthy of praise, think about these things.'

And if you were to ask me the straightforward question, 'What is my understanding of a Christian vision in education?', then I think I could do no better than set before you this text and request that you do precisely what it urges us to do – that is, as one translation puts it, to 'think on' these things.

Quality and excellence

I want therefore this morning to focus our attention on two words – quality and excellence. But before going any further let me say a very real word of thanks and appreciation to all of you for the tremendous contribution which you as head teachers make to our Church schools and through you to your staff members and the many others who are involved in and with the life of our schools, and on whom we depend, for their life and well-being.

Quite by coincidence I noticed right on the front page of last week's Tablet the title 'Beacons of Hope – The Role of Church

Schools in Inner Cities'. It was an article reflecting the broad contents of a recent report from the Roman Catholic Bishops of England and Wales – *A Struggle for Excellence*, a report which contains the experiences of twenty-seven head teachers and their staff working in Roman Catholic secondary schools in some of the poorest areas of Britain. In fact it could, I suspect, have been equally well a report about Anglican Church schools not only in the poorest areas but more generally throughout the land. You will perhaps recognize echoes of your own experience in a brief extract from that article:

> OFSTED Inspectors give the schools much praise for educating the whole person. The Inspectors describe them as caring Christian communities with effective pastoral systems, which stress 'personal and collective responsibility within a Christian framework' . . . without exception schools were commended for the creation of 'very orderly and positively working' atmospheres, and the report contains striking evidence of the commitment of Head teachers and their staff. Most schools have high and consistent expectations of their pupils, whom they encouraged to take their share of responsibility for their own learning, in an attempt to build up a strong sense of individual purpose and direction . . . more than half the schools in the study receive high praise from OFSTED Inspectors for the level of education they provide and the verdict on the vast majority is favourable.

This certainly reflects something not only of my own impressions but of my own direct experience. For throughout my episcopate, and now as Archbishop of York, I have taken a particular interest in schools and in education generally, making frequent visits to schools. It was during the course of one such visit to a secondary school in North Yorkshire, a first rate-school I might add, where at the conclusion of the visit I was presented with a fine silver ink stand – certainly a beautiful and valuable object. There seemed to be some amusement during the actual presentation. It turned out that it had in fact been presented some ninety years ago to the Archbishop of York, Cosmo Gordon Lang, when he had visited, but he had forgotten to take it with him. I did not forget. It is now safely in my home at Bishopthorpe.

I began by setting before you a text from Paul's Letter to the Philippians and drew attention to two words in particular – 'quality' and 'excellence' – as being characteristic in my view of a Christian view of education. They are words which are almost in danger of becoming jargon and which perhaps we need to recover in terms of their practical outworking. Other fine sounding phrases are often used – 'moral and spiritual values' is one – but what we need to ask ourselves, I think, is more about how these can be appreciated, absorbed, internalized within the individual and within the community life of the school as a whole, than about whether they can be delivered on some kind of platter.

The heart of education

Any Christian view for education must surely have as its very heart and centre something about quality and excellence in terms of the school as a community.

I say this because at the very heart of our faith is the mystery of God – God the Holy Trinity, and if we believe each of us is created in the image and likeness of God and that our communities, our society, our world are called to reflect something of the divine life, then our insight into the very nature and being of God the Holy Trinity is the essential key to our being and belonging together in community.

The school is called to reflect these qualities: a fellowship and community which gives individuals scope fully to be themselves, yet participating equally in the common life. Furthermore, to stress that the school is a community of persons (reflecting the Trinitarian life) is to emphasize relationships; the personal is thus prior to the institutional; the institutional exists not for its own sake but solely for the purpose of nurturing and sustaining the relations of the persons who comprise any particular community or organization. Thus I believe there are here serious questions for us all about the structures, the framework, the rules which can and will and do best promote quality and excellence in relationship between staff and students, between and among students, between and among staff, including the head. In other words, there will need to be some clear expression of the community's own self-understanding and how practically this can be realized, and the structures and organization which can and will best do this, with all involved as living, lively, and dynamic partners. Here is a vision of a school which stresses neither the individual at the expense of the whole nor the whole at the expense of the individual, but where, in seeking the best in their being and belonging for each person, there is equally the quest for quality and excellence in the nature of relationships throughout the whole school community, so that interdependence and interrelatedness characterize the nature of the school itself. So how can such a vision be effected? What are those bonds of interdependence and interconnectedness which bind a school community together and give it a sense of identity, of purpose and of direction?

Worship and prayer

I well recognize of course that each school will necessarily have its own particular ethos and flavour, its own identity and characteristics born of its own story, history and present circumstances. But within the school itself and between our Church secondary schools what are the features which bind us together as members one of another – the Body of Christ?

In my view, one necessary prerequisite of quality and excellence, deriving immediately from what I have been saying about God and the Holy Trinity, is worship and prayer. Here surely is a binding force among us – the gift and the grace of God the Holy Spirit.

I believe that every Church secondary school has a real opportunity and responsibility to provide for every pupil a daily act of worship which will be imaginative, creative and engaging and so will enable thoughtful and careful reflection. I am well aware that the constraints of some buildings simply do not allow the whole school to gather in this way, though where that is possible I should certainly wish to encourage it. But there are other ways of arranging such events – by houses, in year groups, even in the classroom. However it is arranged such a gathering ought to make possible an atmosphere of some spiritual depth where the presence of God is acknowledged and celebrated.

I believe there is still much to be garnered from the type of assembly/morning prayer, or however it may be described, which does have some basic and predictable and disciplined framework about it. A story, a hymn and a prayer you might retort somewhat scornfully. Nevertheless, I do believe we need to be paying far greater attention to spiritual awakening and formation, to promoting spiritual growth and nurture, than perhaps we have done hitherto and that there is much in the Christian tradition upon which to draw.

The morning assembly makes as it were a transition – it celebrates both a moment of arrival and a movement at the beginning of a new day. Quality rather than quantity is clearly to be preferred – and in the course of my episcopal ministry in Wakefield, London and now in York, I have actually participated in some very lively and thought provoking 'thought for the day'-type presentations in just such a context with some moments as well for recollection and reflection – such contributions coming both from staff and students.

I believe too that we owe it to our students to teach them to pray. There are some very attractive collections of prayers – both new and old, ancient and modern. I could hardly believe it when in one school I was about to embark on the Lord's Prayer when the head whispered in my ear, 'I don't think they will know it!' But why? To some extent prayer is learned by sheer repetition – not in a wooden and matter of fact kind of way, but certainly by repetition which breeds familiarity and the sense of making the prayer one's own, perhaps for example using one particular prayer daily throughout one term.

There are prayers too which have been prayed by women and men in all manner of situations and circumstances which form part of the continuing Christian story and whose story could actually issue in prayer. Again, the Scriptures themselves I believe are still a rich treasure house for reading and for story, for poetry and for song; there is a huge quarry of Christian literature including, for example the lives of the saints great and small. We need to engage in a lively and imaginative way with the tradition. We owe it to our young people to ensure that they gradually imbibe these deep down resources, so that in times of darkness and despair, in times of difficulty and crisis, as well as in joy and thanksgiving, they have within them these riches upon which to draw. Who knows they might even spontaneously resort to prayer! I have already mentioned the Lord's Prayer and will be very relieved when not only our own Church but the Churches together have settled on one single version which can be used ecumenically.

Students might also be encouraged to compose and use their own prayers. I have seen this done to very great effect – collections of prayers exhibited in the same way as collections of poems and other pieces of work. It should be possible too to draw into acts of worship music and dance and drama, poetry and story and silence. And I would hope more attention could be given to the benefits and rewards of simply being together in silence even if only for a sort of two minute silence, if not daily then certainly weekly.

One of the most impressive occasions which certainly has left its mark on me was a visit I made to an evening act of worship at a Quaker school where the whole school – young and old – sat together in silence for fully ten minutes and I think rather longer than that.

Building up connections with the local church and parish and clergy are important and the celebration of the Eucharist in school or the school going to church for a eucharistic celebration can be a very enriching experience. It needs careful preparation, but again I have participated in such events in Church secondary schools in London and have been much impressed by the participatory nature of these occasions and the whole mood and atmosphere of this particular service which itself can be a powerful link between the local parish and parishes and clergy and the school.

Christianity and other faiths

Now I well recognize that there are here considerable sensitivities with regard to those of other faiths. I would, however, in this connection make two points. The first is that those of other faiths do not actually thank us for being apologetic or unsure or uncertain of our own, or even attempting to play down the differences or distinctiveness of our respective faith traditions. Secondly it is very significant that many people from other faith traditions make a deliberate choice to send their children to a Church school precisely because it does have some faith, life and tradition. Our Christian faith, life and teaching ought certainly to be overt without ever being oppressive. Indeed I have in mind here the words of Francis of Assisi: 'Go and preach the gospel but with words if you must.' There's a challenge for every Church secondary school!

Certainly one of the great contrasts for me personally, having moved from the Diocese of London to the Diocese of York, has been the very much smaller presence of those of other faiths in schools in the York Diocese, whereas regularly in London in many of our Church aided schools I found often some 70–80 per cent Muslim children, many of whose parents had, as I have already hinted, particularly opted for a self-consciously Christian school.

In this context, there is a passage from one of the pastoral letters of the last Lambeth Conference – that ten-yearly gathering of Anglican Bishops worldwide which may be of some help and assistance. The letter itself is significantly entitled, *Sharing the Hospitality of God*:

> Part of our hospitality to people from a variety of backgrounds will be the welcoming of those of other faiths. We know that God has not left himself without witnesses anywhere (Acts 14.17). This enables us to a firmer degree of commonality with people of other faiths. At the same time Jesus Christ is for us the definitive apprehension of the divine; and we continue to hold firmly to our conviction that in him God has revealed himself uniquely.

Of course we need to know about and respect those of other faiths, but we shall never really enter into the faith experience of the world's religions unless we actually take the trouble to be with and alongside them. Whenever I make a visit to Jerusalem, for example, I always make a point of going to the Western Wall, of spending some time in the Mosque as well as sitting quietly by the entrance to the Damascus Gate – and yes of course spending time in the great Constantinian Basilica of the Anastasis.

There are commonalities to be shared and celebrated – commonalities which have their very *fons et origo* in the being of the one eternal God. We should do well to concentrate some of our attention on these. Yet no one can avoid and evade either the differences or the central claims which the Christian faith makes about the final and definitive and unique nature of the incarnation of God – God in Jesus Christ.

Spiritual and moral values

I have spoken about quality and excellence in relation to the school as a community of persons; and in terms of worship and prayer; for the Church school there must also be a particular concern about spiritual and moral values. The word 'spiritual' is itself somewhat elusive and can be very deceptive. Furthermore, in attempting to define it, we need to beware and proceed with some caution, lest in attempting to define it we actually undermine the very thing it is about and is attempting to communicate. Again, I begin to be very wary when there is talk of spirituality – or the 'spiritual' with little reference to very much else – as indeed I am with the use of the word 'moral'. It was one of my distinguished predecessors, William Temple, who when he became Archbishop of Canterbury, seems to have been responsible for introducing into the preamble of the 1944 Education Act this word 'spiritual' rather than the word 'religious'. It was, you will no doubt be aware, as a result of considerable negotiation and hard bargaining that the Act itself was forged on the basis of a partnership of interest between Church and State. Temple himself commented: 'The real significance of the Education Act 1944 is that it was born, not as all its predecessors were, in an atmosphere of bitter religious conflict, but as a result of partnership between State, the education authorities, the teachers, the Church and the churches.' And I suppose if he were saying that today he would undoubtedly have added – of the other faith communities.

Temple's wise and careful use of the word 'spiritual' in preference to 'religious' at once indicated a somewhat broader and altogether more tolerant tone – a deliberate attempt to be inclusive rather than exclusive, which typified Temple's understanding and interpretation of the purposes of the Act itself.

Already, as I have hinted, I am extremely loath to separate off, to single out, the spiritual and the moral from all the rest of what we understand about education. There is a real sense in which the spiritual and moral ought to be the yeast in the dough, interpenetrating every aspect of life in school and in society for that matter. For surely any consideration of spiritual and moral values must imply some understanding of who and what we are – the question of the Psalmist (8.4) and of so many others: 'What is man, that thou art mindful of him?' Perhaps, as a primary task we ought to be exploring some of the images and themes about the nature of our being human among which I suspect it may be possible to discover some common strands and themes across ideological borders and which from the roots of a shared insight into the nature of our common humanity we could then go on to draw out some shared understandings about the spiritual and moral, but very much as part of our insight into the integrity and wholeness of what it is to be human. Thus the spiritual and the moral cannot simply be achieved on the principle of 'add-on' – they are fundamental to the whole enterprise.

And just as the question is being posed more widely in the nation – What kind of society do we want? – so there is a similar and prior question to be asked about the essential purpose of education and the nature of the school as a community. Is the whole purpose of the school simply to deliver the curriculum? At all costs to ensure a decent place in the league tables? There must surely be more to life than league tables! Is it to equip people with the utilitarian, economic and social skills they will need in the world of work? Or is it to help them grow and develop as persons, thus equipping them for a fulfilled life of continuing growth and development and formation which enables them to make a contribution of themselves as persons to the wider community and society? I believe that Schumacher had it right in his book, *Small is Beautiful*, when he wrote:

> The problems of education are merely reflections of the deepest problems of our age. They cannot be solved by organization, administration or the expenditure of money, even though the importance of all these is not to be denied. We are suffering from a metaphysical disease and the cure therefore must be metaphysical. Education which fails to clarify our central convictions is mere training or indulgence. For it is our central convictions which are in disorder, and, as long as the present anti-metaphysical temper exists, the disease will grow worse. Education, far from ranking as our greatest resource will then be an agent of our destruction.

We may not agree with the dire prediction of this last sentence. Nevertheless, he takes us back to the very fundamental question which I raised just now about what it is to be human, how we understand ourselves and our lives, and included in all of that there must surely be both spiritual and moral dimensions. A Japanese engineer and businessman was once asked at a conference on education what he believed the main purpose of education was. After quite some pause, he replied that the central and overriding purpose of education was 'making good people'.

One of the great strengths of our Anglican tradition in particular is the way in which it seeks to hold together every aspect of life and living. *Holy Living* and *Holy Dying* are the titles of two works by Jeremy Taylor, bishop and theologian in the seventeenth century. *The Whole Duty of Man* is another title from the same Caroline period. Spirituality and morality and the values which emerge from them are not just one part of the enterprise, they are the very enterprise itself. It is impossible to speak of a human person, of society, of ourselves as a community of persons, without recourse both to the spiritual and the moral.

Moreover, I simply cannot see how it is possible to proceed in what is described by some to be a value free or morally neutral context. For surely any time a teacher says 'Johnny don't do that', or to be more realistic these days, 'Johnny I don't think it is a very good idea if you do that!', then at once such statements presuppose surely some kind of moral framework and code. We should not be shy or coy about setting before our pupils some of the more elusive yet challenging statements made by Jesus as they are recorded in the New Testament.

The Ten Commandments were in the news not all that long ago in spite of one newspaper having taken the clergy to task, then itself getting them wrong. They are not unlike a wide range of such codes in the ancient world – but they still encapsulate the most profound moral wisdom. For I take it that we are all still agreed that murder is wrong; stealing is wrong; lying is wrong; the honouring of mother and father is to be encouraged and so on. In any case as one of my distinguished predecessors, Archbishop Stuart Blanch, wrote in a very useful little book on the Ten Commandments: 'The Commandments are not a series of regulations designed to make us good or to make us happy or even to control our vices. They are intimately associated with an experience of the ineffable God, the creator of the Universe, the Lord and Master of all life.'

One of the ways in which spiritual and moral values may be expressed and embodied in a school is, I would suggest, in the school rules or whatever such provision may be termed. It ought to be very evident in any such framework what the expectations are in terms of behaviour, courtesy, civility, concern for each other; and whilst I should not wish too much to overload any such set of rules or regulations, nevertheless, the contract or covenant made between school and pupil ought to be such that it will both enshrine such values and enable them to flourish. Furthermore, the positive inclusion of students themselves in the framing of such provisions, as well as in their application in the school, will surely be a powerful means of assisting them to appreciate that as well as rights to be safeguarded there are duties and responsibilities to be undertaken. I have been very impressed in a number of schools I have visited in which students themselves are actually included in the disciplinary processes and where the judgement of one's peers is often somewhat more threatening and severe than that of the staff even or the head!

I would have thought too that it is in this area of the moral and the spiritual where the roots and wellsprings of effective and successful pastoral care are to be discerned, where the concerns for justice, an approach to special needs and equal rights are best located.

Any Christian educational establishment will seek quality and excellence in all these areas and not least, arising out of the general thrust of the Gospels, a special care for the marginalized, the misfit, the maverick. I dare to hope too that Paul's reflections on the gifts of the Holy Spirit might figure somewhere in any consideration of the ethos and environment of the school. Where, for example, are those qualities evident which are signs of the presence of the Holy Spirit? How might such counter-cultural qualities be the more fostered and encouraged – compassion, kindness, lowliness, meekness, forbearance, long-suffering, patience (Colossians 3.12; Ephesians 4.2)?

The role of the school building

It was Archbishop William Temple in his book, *Christianity and Social Order*, who whilst writing about the life of the school as a living community went on to make some further comments about school buildings:

> Now for a good many years the authorities have also begun to see the real perspectives in this matter and some are taking pains to make school buildings not only commodious and beautiful . . . there is still room for a great deal of development in this direction but our feet are set on the right way.

His comments are of course a reminder, if we should need any such reminder, that our faith is incarnational – that not only do people matter but so does our physical environment. Buildings can and do have a very considerable impact and effect upon us all. And that goes for school buildings par excellence. Furthermore, being the son of a builder I find that I have a particular interest in and eye for not only shape and design, but for quality and excellence in the buildings themselves – and I have visited some pretty extraordinary buildings in my time!

What does the place look like – from the outer approaches? What about the noticeboard (if there is one) and the entrance? Is it clear how you get in? The vestibule area of the school is a key area. At once, a visitor like myself has an immediate impression. Indeed with relation to one school which I know well and which has just endured an OFSTED inspection, one of the key comments and recommendations has been, in my view quite properly, to reshape/order/design the entrance area. As with church buildings I well recognize that there is not always a great deal of room for manoeuvre either financially or in terms of the existing layout or in terms of extravagance of design. But I do believe that it is always possible to make some modest steps in the right direction. And the fact that we may well be faced with a pretty impossible situation ought not to deter us from doing something, however modest that might seem to be. In one of the very worst school buildings I have ever visited in the Diocese of London I remember a very considerable difference had been made by the decision to make a start on painting the main staircase in an altogether brighter and lighter colour. That had an immediate effect on that part of the staircase with regard to behaviour, litter and so on. On the face of it, it was a pretty negligible contribution. Actually, it was a very significant sign and symbol already beginning to make a difference. I recognize also that school buildings are subject to controls about size and space. But I would always want to plead for 'space' – for areas where you do not feel hemmed in or cooped up or whatever. The building – its nature and shape – is a vital element in the equation when we speak of the spiritual.

I mentioned a moment or two ago the entrance area. For any Church school I would hope that it would be possible at once to notice that it was a Christian school with some Christian symbol clearly evident – a cross or a painting or an icon or some such object. And similarly too around the school, perhaps even in each classroom, there might be some unifying outward and visible sign and symbol reproduced in every place – perhaps the same symbol as is in the entrance hall and which quite naturally meets the eye – also displayed at various key points around the school where again it will naturally meet the eye. And along with any mission statement, which again I notice often displayed in key places, perhaps alongside that, a short prayer.

Now I am aware that in attempting to set before you my thoughts and reflections on today's theme much has been left unsaid. I have concentrated my remarks on a number of more particular aspects of a Church school, which are obviously not the whole story. For the aspirations to quality and excellence must be sought in every aspect of the schools' life and being – not least in the teaching and teaching staff. The style, qualities, personal appearance and attitudes of all who are entrusted with this responsibility are important. For as is sometimes remarked of the Christian faith itself – it is caught not taught – I recall from my own schooldays that there were many unspoken qualities which I believe I caught at an early age from my teachers and for which I remain thankful.

Leadership and a sense of direction

Finally, to all of you has been entrusted the task of leadership. This is a subject in itself. Yet I am mindful too of particular Christian insights into the concept of leadership which are plainly evident throughout the Scriptures – servant, shepherd, steward, episcopos are all identified in John Finney's *Understanding Leadership*, and which I believe would merit further enquiry and study. In a more general context I have myself been much helped by John Adair's *Not Bosses but Leaders*. Indeed when I first went to the Diocese of Wakefield I took the opportunity of taking my staff meeting members, about seven of them in all, off to St George's House, Windsor for a consultation on precisely this theme. I still remember the points which John Adair put to us all as the characteristics of a high performance team and I think they are worth sharing with you now. A high performance team, he writes, has the following characteristics: clear realistic objectives, a shared sense of purpose, best use of resources, an atmosphere of openness; it reviews progress, builds on experience, and rides out storms.

Above all surely leadership is about giving people a sense of direction, of inspiring them with a clarity of vision and purpose for the whole enterprise. To this end given your own clear responsibilities as team leaders and team builders, you must surely be in the business of creating a high performance team. Yet in so doing be careful to ensure that you keep in touch with the grass roots – or perhaps more appropriately the chalk face.

I began with a text from Paul's Letter to the Philippians which drew our attention to purity, beauty, graciousness, justice, loveliness and excellence – with the request that we 'think on' these things. I very much hope you will continue yourselves to 'think on' these things as the clear characteristics of any Christian vision for education. Above all, I conclude with St Irenaeus: 'The glory of God is a person fully alive.' Pray God that our Church schools may continue in this vocation – the making of persons 'fully alive' to the praise and glory of God.

The Church in education: where do we go from here?

Canon John Hall

I began teaching, in 1971, in a County high school in Hull. I was by no means convinced that Church schools were necessary. Would it not be better for the Church to put its efforts into schools like mine? We could avoid the charge of elitism (often levelled at the time) and make an effective Christian contribution to the comprehensive system of education. These were unconscious echoes of a debate in the Methodist Church eighty years earlier which had led to a decision to hand over their schools. Perhaps my thoughts largely arose in 1971 from a reading of the recently published Durham Report, *The Fourth R*. My doubts were clearly shared by many, although the Durham Report held the line against the abolition of Church schools. In 1971, I could be excused for thinking that the Church of England should have confidence about its access to County schools. Although there are many Christians working in County schools and many clergy visiting, governing, sometimes even leading worship in County schools, the picture has changed dramatically in the last thirty years. Access is now largely denied. My conviction of the need for Church schools has increased over the intervening years as the opportunity for Christian influence on County schools has progressively decreased.

This article began life in 1995, when I was director of education for the Diocese of Blackburn, as a paper for the bishops of the north-west region meeting with their wives at Whalley Abbey. My thoughts about the purpose and provision of Church schools had been focused by the need to prepare for a Blackburn Diocesan

Synod debate that year. I refer to the report published for that debate by Blackburn Diocesan Board of Education under the title *Our Heritage: their Future* later in this article. The title of the report could equally serve as a sub-title for this article.

The Church of England has a substantial stake in the English educational system but development has been largely haphazard and unplanned. The Church of England educates one in eight pupils in maintained schools, more than 900,000 altogether. But there is a disparity between provision at primary and secondary level. One primary school in four is Church of England but only one secondary school in twenty. Only one primary school in ten is voluntary aided Church of England. Voluntary schools of all kinds represent more than one primary school in three and one secondary school in five. The overwhelming majority of those not provided by the Church of England are Roman Catholic, with a few Methodist or Jewish schools, and now two Muslim schools and one Seventh Day Adventist school, with a handful provided by secular trusts.

The 1944 Education Act introduced the possibility of Church schools submitting to the control of the local education authority (LEA) in return for full funding. The Dioceses of London, Southwark and Blackburn opted for voluntary aided rather than voluntary controlled status. A number of other dioceses opted for controlled status but in most cases the decisions were left to the parishes.

During 1995, a task group in the Diocese of Blackburn commissioned research into the provision and spread of Church schools across the diocese. The research was published in a report, *Our Heritage: their Future*. Blackburn has almost 160 voluntary aided (more than any other diocese) and 30 voluntary controlled schools. On average across the diocese, 29 per cent of children in primary schools are in Church of England schools. This average cloaks a wide disparity in local provision: from the north of the diocese, where three out of four children of primary school age are in Church of England schools, to the Fylde coast, where only one primary pupil out of eight is in a Church of England school. At secondary level too, there is little evidence of effective planning. Only one secondary pupil out of eight in Lancashire is in a Church of England school. Large tracts of the diocese, particularly in the far east and far west, are bereft of Church of England secondary education. By contrast, at both primary and secondary phases, 18 per cent of school children in Lancashire are in Roman Catholic schools.

I suggest that, while the Church of England may find it difficult to plan for coherent development of the provision of Church schools, there is now an opportunity and need to do so. Church schools are strongly established and many of them are successful and popular. If the Church is to argue for and support coherent change, it must be on the basis of a clear perception of the purpose and value of Church schools.

What Church schools are for

Historical provision of Church schools

When the National Society was founded in 1811, schools in union with the Society were to provide education in accordance with the rites, practices and doctrines of the Church of England. The Trust Deeds of Church of England schools continue to make the same requirement.

Within forty years of the foundation of the National Society, at the time of the religious census of 1851, there were 17,015 National (i.e. Church of England) schools with nearly 956,000 pupils. There were 1,500 Free Church schools with 225,000 pupils and a similar number of Roman Catholic schools. Before the establishment of the universal system of education in 1870, there was widespread discussion of the future provision and wide-spread disparity of views about the relationship of Church and State. There were groups within the Church of England and many in the Free Churches who opposed the receipt of any government grant for Church schools. On the other hand there were many outside the Churches arguing for a system of education entirely provided by the State.

In 1870, with the establishment of school boards and universal elementary education, the new board schools were free to decide whether to offer religious instruction. Although they were established to balance the Churches' provision, most offered non-denominational but nevertheless clearly Christian religious instruction. Financial provision favoured board schools until the Education Act of 1902 established Local Education Authorities and put Church schools on a better financial footing. The Free Churches had by then decided to hand over their schools to the local authorities and objected strongly to State funding for Church schools, in particular Roman Catholic schools. The objection to 'Rome on the rates' caught the public mood and led to the election of a Liberal Government which in 1906 published a bill to abolish State funding for Church schools. The Churches fought back vigorously. Public meetings were held all over the country. Bishop Knox of Manchester led a parliamentary lobby. Thirty-six trainloads of men from Lancashire joined him. The House of Lords subjected the Bill to death by a thousand cuts and the Government eventually abandoned the legislation.

The Education Act 1944

By the Second World War, Church schools, long under-funded by the Church for repair and development, required substantial capital investment that the Church could not afford. Many Church schools were run down and unpopular. The historic agreement between the Churches and Government, as the Archbishop of York has suggested, depended on and foreshadowed real partnership. It led to two new categories of school. The voluntary controlled school, provided by its foundation, would be controlled by the LEA. The voluntary aided school, provided and controlled by its foundation, would be assisted by Government grants to cover half the capital costs. Both kinds of school would be fully maintained by the LEA. This '1944 settlement', of course, persists, retains the support of the Church and is re-stated in the new School Standards and Framework Act. The key difference for schools which came under the control of the LEA under the 1944 Act was that all the teachers would be appointed by the LEA without religious test, except for a number up to one fifth of the staff, so-called reserved teachers, who could deliver denominational religious instruction where the parents so requested. The expectation was that agreed syllabus religious instruction would be given on three mornings, with Church teaching on the other two.

The agreed syllabus was a further result of the 1944 settlement. Religious instruction and collective worship were to be compulsory in all, not just Church, schools. Parents would have the right to withdraw their children. The syllabus would be agreed by a new Agreed Syllabus Conference of which the Church of England constituted one of the four committees with a right of veto, the other committees representing the Free Churches, the teachers and the LEA.

These developments constituted a considerable extension for the influence of the Church of England into every aspect of the English school system. No longer was influence confined to the schools provided by the Church. Every school would have Christian religious instruction and Christian worship and the Church of England would be at the heart of agreeing what should be taught. The first syllabuses agreed under the system, whilst not reflecting any particular denomination, were nevertheless highly Christian, biblical and confessional, teaching Christianity from within, as true, not from without, as the opinion held by some. The loss of control of so many Church of England schools in the wake of the 1944 Act may seem now a considerable reversal of the Church's influence. It must have seemed a fair bargain at the time.

The question 'what were Church schools for?' in 1944, when Christian education was to be provided in all schools, seemed less important than it had been a hundred years earlier when the Churches were the only providers but denominational rivalry was intense. The answer was to provide Church teaching for those children whose parents wanted it.

A *survey of religious instruction: 1960*

If there were high expectations of the impact of religious instruction in all kinds of schools in 1944, it might be appropriate to ask whether such high expectations were fulfilled. In 1960 Hugh Pollard, later to be the first principal of St Martin's College Lancaster but then at the University of Sheffield Institute of Education, undertook a survey into the biblical knowledge and religious attitudes of 15-year-olds. The research broke down results between modern, technical and grammar schools. None of them were Church schools. Knowledge of the Old Testament was regarded as scant with fewer than half the grammar school pupils being able to name a prophet. While answers to simple questions about the life of Jesus were quite good, only a quarter of the sample knew what was celebrated at Whitsuntide and answers to questions about the early Church were poor.

The survey report proposed improving the specialized training of RI teachers and simplifying the Agreed Syllabuses. However, the level of simplification may be judged by the proposed inclusion of teaching about Sheshbazzar, Gnosticism and the Arminians. It might be of interest to add that the report publishes figures of religious practice amongst those sampled. The group with the lowest level of religious observance was, predictably, that of boys at secondary modern schools and the group with the highest level was that of girls at grammar schools. But two thirds of the secondary modern boys claimed to pray on their own and some-times to attend church. Almost all the grammar school girls claimed to pray on their own and to attend church from time to time. Regular church attendance was claimed by a quarter of the secondary modern boys and over half the grammar school girls.

By 1968, when the Inner London Education Authority published their new Agreed Syllabus, 'Learning for Life', much had changed. The influence of Piaget and Ronald Goldman was clear. RE was to be delivered in the primary school through themes accessible to the children, such as 'light', 'stars', 'the wind', 'pets', and 'friends'. Nevertheless the syllabus was almost exclusively Christian and confessional (though non-denominational) in its purpose. It is not clear how far the new syllabus was delivered in practice. There is little inspection evidence available.

The Durham Commission: 1970

The Church of England's position on religious instruction and on Church schools was reviewed by a commission, established in 1967 by the Church of England Board of Education and the National Society, chaired by Bishop Ian Ramsey of Durham. Views about Church schools and about religious instruction, as about so many things, had changed through the previous decade. Challenges were being made from all quarters, not least from within the Church, to compulsory religious instruction and school worship. Grammar schools were being abolished and the comprehensive ideal, one school for all, was persuading many to support the abolition of Church schools. The commission took evidence from a wide range of interests. Amongst them, the Headmasters' Conference, the Headmasters' Association and the National Association of Head Teachers made a joint submission, suggesting that religious instruction should not be timetabled but that religious education should emerge through the general provision of education in the school. The commission published its report, *The Fourth R*, in 1970.

They were not persuaded that religion should be excluded from the timetable but saw the unpopularity of the statutory basis for religious instruction and worship. The report recommended an attempt to preserve religious education ('RE' now, not 'RI') and school worship for all pupils, through discontinuing the statutory provisions of the 1944 Act and abolishing agreed syllabuses. It was proposed that there should be 'some degree of statutory acknowledgement with regard to RE and worship' perhaps based on the spiritual and moral education obligations in the 1944 Act. It was not clear what might constitute this new 'statutory acknowledgement'. On the other hand where RE was timetabled it should have two periods a week and where included with other subjects should receive similar weighting. Each LEA should have a 'handbook of suggestions' for RE teachers and be urged to appoint an adviser for RE. A need was seen for more qualified RE teachers and for suitable and up-to-date curriculum materials. These proposals would have removed the Church of England's influence on County schools.

Whilst the Durham Commission did not support the abolition of Church schools, they responded to the public controversy by proposing the reduction in the Church's influence on them and the gradual reduction in the numbers of voluntary aided schools. Withdrawal from the so-called Dual System (i.e. partnership with the LEA in the provision of Church schools) was regarded as undesirable or in any case impracticable. However, voluntary aided schools in areas where they were the only school accessible to their community should consider a change to controlled status. RE in aided schools should be subject to inspection by HM Inspectorate, in other words presumably should cease to be denominational in character. Aided schools' admission policies should give priority to children in the local area without reference to denominational allegiance and national and local working parties should be set up without delay to examine ways and means of ecumenical co-operation within the Dual System. An urgent need was seen for a commission to review the financing of Church schools and Church colleges.

The Commission's view of the purpose of Church schools reflected that of 1944.

> It is extremely important to recognise at the outset that the C of E voluntary school of today is an institution whose roots go back into a past where its role was seen as twofold. It was general, to serve the nation through its children, and domestic, to equip the children of the Church to take their places in the Christian community.

It may seem, however, that the general purpose, as opposed to the domestic purpose, was now paramount and all the points of distinctiveness of the voluntary aided school were to be abandoned save the power for the governors or managers to appoint the staff.

The impact of the Durham Report was important throughout the seventies as questions continued to be asked about the role of Church schools. Many voluntary aided schools were re-built; a number became voluntary controlled under the pressure of cost, although the contribution made by the governors of voluntary aided schools towards capital costs reduced progressively from 50 per cent to 25 per cent and finally to 15 per cent. However, the statutory changes to Church schools and to religious education which the Durham Report sought were never implemented.

The impact of the last ten years

The statutory changes that did eventually occur imposed a positive central influence on RE and served to entrench Church schools more thoroughly than before.

The National Curriculum had been discussed by the Prime Minister (Mr, now Lord, Callaghan) in the months before the general election of 1979 but was not implemented until the Education Reform Act 1988. RE was omitted from the National (centrally prescribed) Curriculum but made part of the school's basic curriculum and prescribed for all pupils in school, from Year R to Year 13. Moreover, under the Education Act 1993, LEAs were required to reconvene their standing advisory council for RE and an agreed syllabus conference and to agree a new local syllabus based on the national guidelines produced by the School Curriculum and Assessment Authority (later replaced by the Qualifications and Curriculum Authority).

Before these developments, despite the best endeavours of many, RE had not been strongly established. It was often omitted from the curriculum entirely, certainly for pupils over the age of fourteen, and, where taught, ill-regarded in the secondary school and, in the primary school, frequently lost as a theme within an integrated day. For example, in 1987 a survey of primary schools in Gloucester revealed that only 15 per cent of the County schools surveyed had developed their own schemes of work for RE and two thirds of County schools had no separate timetabled period for RE, teaching it through an integrated approach. The picture in many Church schools was not much better. Three quarters of the small sample of voluntary aided Church of England schools surveyed had no timetabled RE.

The introduction of the National Curriculum and the new syllabuses for RE has meant that RE is required to be timetabled in all schools for all pupils. It is afforded 5 per cent of curriculum time. A new short-course GCSE recently introduced has meant that 14- to 16-year-olds are able to study RE 5 per cent of the time with the prospect of a qualification. Where RE is well taught, it is seen as a popular subject with a significant contribution to make to the intellectual development of pupils as well as their spiritual and moral development.

These improvements for RE might seem at first sight a considerable advantage from the Church's point of view. But RE has changed its emphasis over the years and is now unrecognizable from the point of view of the legislators in 1944 or that of the Durham Commission in 1970. RE, in County schools, is no longer Christianity taught as true, from within the household of faith. It gives predominance to Christianity, but embraces the five other major world religions. This is a proper and understandable development, which takes belief seriously and treats each religion separately. But time will tell what impression of religion and the influence of religion is left in an adolescent mind trying to retain details of the belief and its impact on religious practice and moral attitudes of the six major word religions. Agreed Syllabus RE will enable pupils to learn about religion and to learn from religion. It will make a contribution to their spiritual and moral development as well as their intellectual development. But it will not be an education in religion and therefore not truly Christian education.

RE has a different emphasis when it is taught in accordance with a diocesan syllabus, i.e. in a voluntary aided school or in a voluntary controlled school where reserved teachers (or others) are willing and able to deliver it and where the parents have requested Church teaching. There, Christianity will be taught from within throughout the school experience. The faith of the Christian community of the Church will be explicitly and legitimately acknowledged as 'our faith' even where individual teachers and pupils will not be at the same point of making the faith of the community their own personal faith. This is not indoctrination but a recognition of the faith on which the school is founded and the community to which the school belongs. It offers the pupil a proper basis against which to make personal decisions about faith, at the age at which such decisions are made. It is, of course, right to ensure that pupils have a proper acquaintance with other faiths than Christianity. This acquaintance both enables their understanding of the impact of faith on life and also develops understanding and respect for those of faiths other than their own.

The new system for the inspection of schools, introduced in 1992 over a four-year cycle, allowing the separate inspection of certain aspects of Church schools, has led to real improvements in education. Denominational inspection, under Section 13 of the Education (Schools) Act 1992 (Section 23 of the consolidated act in 1996), has taken place alongside the OFSTED inspection, the two inspection processes looking jointly at the spiritual, moral, social and cultural development of pupils. This has led to the increased importance of these issues in all schools and in particular in voluntary controlled and some voluntary aided schools. The denominational inspection of worship has led especially in voluntary controlled schools to many Church of England schools looking afresh at the contemporary implications of that historical link.

The position of Church schools has been further strengthened in recent years as a result of the changes made in the relationship between schools and LEAs by local management of schools (LMS). Church schools, like other schools, have ceased to be under the effective control of LEAs and have had enough financial flexibility to acquire the services they need from the LEA or the diocesan authority or indeed elsewhere. This practical impact of the previous Government's rhetoric about choice and diversity, not rescinded by the present Government, has enabled Church schools to establish their proper distinctiveness within the system. Many diocesan authorities have been able in consequence to strengthen the level of service they have been able to offer their schools. This virtuous circle looks set to continue.

Again, league tables and levels of oversubscription have led to the recognition by government that many Church schools are both successful and popular with parents. The report, *Our Heritage: their Future*, in the Diocese of Blackburn, referred to earlier, also included research into questions of quality. A small but representative sample of primary and secondary schools had sent an extensive questionnaire to parents, an extended version of that used by OFSTED. It revealed high levels of parental satisfaction. In three widely differing secondary schools, for example, on the basis of a sample of 329 parents of Year 10 pupils, there was almost 100 per cent agreement to the proposition: 'I am happy that the school teaches Christian values.' There was a similar level of positive response to the proposition: 'The school places a clear emphasis on Anglican teaching and worship.' In the primary schools, the parents of Year 6 children were surveyed. The highest levels of satisfaction, very high indeed, were with the propositions: 'I feel that I can approach the school at any time'; 'My child is happy at school' and 'The head teacher is accessible, approachable and helpful.' There were also, for example, high levels of satisfaction with the proposition: 'Christian values are built into the ethos and teaching.' On average in answer to all the questions in the primary schools the 'agree' or 'strongly agree' categories were at 94.1 per cent. Those answers included a comparatively low level of satisfaction with the amount of homework received.

The most recent legislation does nothing to weaken the position of Church schools, quite the reverse. The School Standards and Framework Act 1998 will allow Church schools to make a free choice of category. Voluntary controlled schools were first allowed to opt for the voluntary aided category in 1986 but paying sometimes considerable compensation to the LEA for capital expenditure over the years of LEA control. Under the new Act, voluntary controlled schools will be able to opt for the voluntary aided category paying no compensation at the time of transfer provided that the diocese can guarantee that the governing body will be able to pay 15 per cent of future maintenance and capital costs.

The freedoms of voluntary aided schools to appoint staff whose religious opinions are in accordance with the 'tenets of the Church of England' and whose conduct is not incompatible 'with the tenets or the upholding of the precepts' of the Church are positively stated in the Act. Moreover the Government incorporated in the Act the Church's view that it should be possible to ensure the appointment of head teachers who were 'able and fit to preserve and develop the religious character of the school' for voluntary controlled and foundation Church of England schools. Church schools should be encouraged to use these freedoms to ensure the appointment of staff with a clear commitment to the distinctive character of the school.

Finally, the Government recognizes that diocesan authorities have an important role to play and are significant partners in the support and development of the statutory education system of this country. This recognition is worked out both in the new Act and in the many regulations and codes of practice which serve to give effect to the new legal requirements.

Church schools have perhaps never been in a position so widely respected and so strongly entrenched. The Church and the schools themselves need to use this strength to ensure that they are all fit for their purpose.

So what are Church schools for?

The answer to the question of the purpose of Church schools would now be different from the one given by Archbishop Temple in 1944 or by Bishop Ian Ramsey in 1970. Both assumed that England was broadly a Christian country and that if religious education in all kinds of schools were required to be non-denominational, nevertheless, it would offer a thorough grounding in the fundamentals of the Christian faith. This hope might have been justifiable in the 1940s but it looks a little more threadbare at the end of the 1960s and unsustainable in the 1990s. So another justification for distinctive Church schools emerges to add to those offered by the Durham Report: satisfying the Church's domestic needs; and sustaining an influence in the general system of education nationally. At the end of the twentieth century, many parents who would not regard themselves as part of the household of the Church, but who do want for their children a recognizably Christian education, value the Church's schools and sometimes battle hard for places.

The report *On the Way* (1995) suggested that nationally the Church of England was only in touch with 15 per cent of young people. This disregards the Church's contact through statutory education. In Lancashire, for example, the Churches together educate over half the pupils of primary age and almost a third of those of secondary age. Unless we build on the present position by ensuring that our schools are solidly founded upon Christ and his Gospel, that contact will be more than worthless for the Church; it will be a snare and delusion, inoculating against Christianity rather than letting children catch the faith.

The purpose of Church schools is clear, a purpose which should be fulfilled in voluntary aided schools and elements of which will be possible in voluntary controlled schools as well. Fundamentally, all Church schools should provide a high quality education based on Christian values, enabling pupils to achieve their full God-given potential as human beings for the benefit of God's world. In addition, Church schools should nurture the children of Christian families in the faith of their homes so that it might become for them a living personal faith. And they should offer children of other faiths and none such a positive experience of Christ in his Body the Church that the faith of the Christian community might be respected and understood by them. By God's good grace children with no faith background might also find the seeds planted in them growing into a living personal faith.

Where do we go from here?

Issues of staffing

There are many influences on the character of a school: the governors, the staff, the pupils and their parents, the buildings, the relationships with the local church and community. Under the School Standards and Framework Act, each governing body will be required to make a statement of its school's ethos. But the most powerful influence on the character of the school comes from the beliefs, personality and behaviour of the head teacher. My experience as a new diocesan director of education paying a flying visit to most of the 192 schools in a diocese made this sharply clear. If a school is to have the character identified in the previous section, there can be nothing more important than the appointment of a head teacher committed to the task and able to carry it through. The right, enshrined in section 60 of the 1998 Act, of the governors of a voluntary aided school to make decisions about the appointment of head teachers and of all other teaching staff on the basis of Christian faith and practice has already been mentioned. The practice of appointing reserved teachers for voluntary controlled schools has largely fallen into abeyance. There is no reason why it should not be revived. The legal right to appoint reserved teachers is re-stated in the 1998 Act. Up to one fifth of the teachers in a voluntary controlled or foundation Church of England school can be 'reserved' and in their appointment the same insistence on adherence to the faith and practice of the Church can be applied as in the case of teachers for voluntary aided schools. The new legal position over the appointment of head teachers of voluntary controlled or foundation Church of England schools should allow foundation governors, assisted by diocesan advisers, to ask direct questions at interview. These should probe how the candidates see the Christian character of the school working out in practice and how they might personally contribute to its development.

Christian character

Ultimately the Christian character of the school will depend on the commitment and attitudes of the staff. The encouragement of the Christian vocation to teach is a vital task for the whole Church. This must be coupled with effective training, both initial teacher training and the continuing professional development of teachers, which enables teachers to see how their personal faith can be focused in their teaching career. For Christian education should be delivered through the whole school curriculum, not just through worship or RE. Nor is it simply a matter of the relationships of and between pupils and teachers and the quality of care in the school, which should be characteristic of all schools. In different ways both the Archbishops have made it clear that there is no such thing as value-free education. It is through the taught curriculum, in science, English, history etc., where the content choices made in the schemes of work and the approach taken by the teacher can and do make explicit the underlying beliefs and values of the school. The values underlying the education in a school where Christian teachers can be appointed should be Christian values.

In practice, of course, Church schools properly see themselves in a variety of different ways and have a variety of character and purpose. A voluntary aided school should have an explicitly Christian mission statement. It will have a foundation majority on the governing body, staff appointed against Christian criteria and contracted to the governing body, and an admissions policy giving preference to the children of Christian families as well as diocesan syllabus RE and Christian worship. The opportunity to be distinctively Christian is greater than in a voluntary controlled school or a foundation school, where there is a foundation minority on the governing body, a majority of staff appointed regardless of their faith or religious practice and an LEA admissions policy giving preference to children on a geographical basis. However, even in a voluntary controlled or a foundation Church of England school, the worship will be distinctively Christian, even as the Archbishop of York has suggested distinctively Anglican, and Christian values will pervade the school.

Again, the rural neighbourhood school serving a scattered community will inevitably have a different character from the urban school where there is ample choice between different categories of school. However, with greater mobility and the evidence of some parents driving their children miles to find an appropriate school, the 'single-provision' school need not be so inhibited about its Christian character as was thought necessary in the different world of 1970.

The urban school in a multi-faith area will inevitably have a different character from the heavily oversubscribed suburban Church school. But again, there is evidence that many Muslim parents value, in the absence of Muslim schools, schools where religion is understood and respected and spirituality taken seriously. They will expect the Christian character of the school to be clear. Church schools increasingly see themselves as distinctive from their neighbouring County schools and that distinction is in their Christian character.

he Bishop's Appeal in Blackburn Diocese in 1949 which raised
125,000, equivalent to £3.4 million at today's prices.

here is another possible route for making funds more widely
vailable where they are needed for the provision of more Church
hools. It has recently been remarked that, in a shire county in
e south of England containing two dioceses, one of the dioceses
d no difficulty funding its 15 per cent for a new Church school,
m accumulated Section 554 trust funds, while the other found
mpossible. This is an area of the historic resources of dioceses
ich there has been no attempt to research let alone equalize.
me dioceses have clearly been better served by the closure and
of redundant schools than have others.

here is to be the national planning recommended by the
ham Commission in 1970, especially if there is to be a real
nsion in the provision of Church of England secondary
ols, some means might have to be found for sharing the his-
education resources of dioceses according to need, much as
een done in relation to funds administered by the Church
missioners.

w commission?

eport of the Durham Commission, set up in 1967, was pub-
in 1970 under the title *The Fourth R*. It said:

ly one thing is completely clear: on the subject of
urch schools the Church of England has never had one
erally agreed policy. It certainly has none today (page
).

rted twenty-six years after the 1944 Act. The years since
urth R have been years of considerable change. The
has not been setting the agenda for education. If RE and
schools are stronger or potentially so now more than ever,
only through the work of the Church but through the ini-

Part of the Church's mission

It seems that now, perhaps for the first time since the early nineteenth century, Church schools are almost universally recognized
and valued. The Secretary of State for Education and
Employment, David Blunkett, has said that Church schools have
something extra, which he would like other schools to have as
well. Even in the Church itself there seems to be a widespread
acceptance of the importance of distinctive Church schools.
Parishes should have the confidence to recognize that the Church
school is a significant part of the Church's mission in the parish
and an unrivalled opportunity for positive encounter with the
wider community. Some clergy still regrettably see the Church
school as a drain on their time and energies. The great majority
of clergy have some involvement as a governor or in leading
worship in schools. Whilst this involvement is often of excellent
quality and highly valued, there is not at present enough opportunity through organized training and continuing ministerial
education to develop the necessary skills.

Planning and progress?

In many local authority areas, the support of the Churches for the
LEA and their need for partnership has led to warm co-operation.
There seems to be a lack of rivalry and an understanding of the
distinctiveness of the Church school. The new code of practice on
the relationship between schools and LEAs explicitly mentions
the services provided by diocesan authorities not just for Church
schools but, in a number of aspects, for other schools as well. The
Teacher Training Agency, promoting the new Learning
Programme for Serving Head Teachers, recognizes that Church
authorities might be able to offer helpful support from their experience on values education for head teachers of non-Church
schools.

The 1998 Act gives effect to the Government's commitment to reduction in class sizes at Key Stage 1. This is likely to have a considerable impact beyond the first few years on class sizes at Key Stage 2. The Government recognizes that the implementation of the strategy cannot be at the expense of parental preference at popular schools and has allowed a substantial sum of money for capital development of schools in relation to the class sizes initiative. In the case of voluntary aided schools, government grant will be paid on 100 per cent of the capital costs. In some cases, this will allow popular, oversubscribed Church schools to expand. In addition the Government has made a commitment that LEA reorganization plans should not overall reduce the provision of places at Church schools within the authority.

The demand for places at school will continue to rise to the end of the century and beyond, especially at secondary level where the Church of England is particularly poorly represented. It will perhaps be possible to build on the security and popularity of the Church's position in statutory education and fulfil at last the Durham Report's recommendation 36 about national planning for Church school provision.

> The 'spread' of church voluntary aided schools should so far as may be possible be more rationally distributed, both geographically and within the educational system. To achieve this end a greater degree of centralised co-ordination will be necessary.

The dioceses are theoretically in a position themselves to plan provision centrally. The 1944 and 1973 Education Acts (Section 86 and Section 2 respectively) made it possible for dioceses to claim the proceeds of sale of closed schools to enable provision to be made elsewhere, whether or not the board of education or of finance was the trustee of the school. When rolls were falling in the seventies and eighties and property values were rising, a number of diocesan boards of education were able to establish or

build up significant trust funds for capital work ing schools. Dioceses have been able to make tl about the use of such funds. Under the 1993 lished that it was lawful to use the interest advisory and support staff. In a number of di (under Section 554 of the consolidated Educati been used to pay the whole or part of goverr cent expenditure on capital and maintenance

Planning and service provision at diocesan l easy and some dioceses find it easier than otl appear to have run their Section 554 funds d interest to fund their advice and support s a number of dioceses such services are imposing service charges on the schools. had the power to pay the governors' 15 pe some governing bodies to divert devolve payment of their 15 per cent cost of a d ment project.

The provision of new schools, or even of always possible where it is desirable. S pay the promoter's 15 per cent contri securing 85 per cent grant from the school thereby without affecting th developers of new housing areas can contribution as a matter of planning that large sums of money can be raise amalgamate them on one site but t parochial. In the 1990s, a by no Diocese of Blackburn raised approa new building and, over four years, towards the cost of a relocated sc examples. Dioceses have raised su the past, although perhaps few as tiative of Government, partly but not exclusively out of concern for the moral education of the nation's young people. It is right to consider at this stage whether the Church might be ready for another major review. Then the Church of England would be well placed to estimate the true strengths of the present position and, on that basis, to build to one of greater strength for the Gospel through the changes recently enacted and which will inevitably come in the next few years.

The National Society
A Christian Voice in Education

The National Society (Church of England) for Promoting Religious Education supports everyone involved in Christian education – teachers, school governors, students, parents, clergy, parish and diocesan education teams – with the resources of its RE centres, courses, conferences and archives.

Founded in 1811, the Society was chiefly responsible for setting up the nationwide network of Church schools in England and Wales, and still helps them with legal and administrative advice for headteachers and governors. It was also a pioneer in teacher education through the Church colleges. The Society now provides resources for those responsible for RE and worship in any school, lecturers and students in colleges, and clergy and lay people in parish education. It publishes a wide range of books and booklets and a resource magazine, *Together with Children*.

The National Society is a voluntary body which works in partnership with the Church of England General Synod Board of Education and the Division for Education of the Church of Wales. An Anglican society, it also operates ecumenically, and helps to promote inter-faith education and dialogue through its RE centres.

For further details of the Society or a copy of our current resources catalogue and how you can support the continuing work of the Society, please contact:

The National Society
Church House
Great Smith Street
London SW1P 3NZ

Telephone: 0171-222 1672
Fax: 0171-233 2592
Email: NS@natsoc.org.uk

Values for Church Schools

Peter Shepherd

'Values in Education' is a term currently in vogue and there is a ground swell of opinion to bring values to the forefront of the educational debate in all schools. This book asks whether there are distinctive values that Church schools should identify and adapt, or should they follow the agenda set by the secular world?

Peter Shepherd is Head of Canon Slade School in Bolton and also an Anglican priest.

£4.00   ISBN 0 901819 61 1

Part of the Church's mission

It seems that now, perhaps for the first time since the early nineteenth century, Church schools are almost universally recognized and valued. The Secretary of State for Education and Employment, David Blunkett, has said that Church schools have something extra, which he would like other schools to have as well. Even in the Church itself there seems to be a widespread acceptance of the importance of distinctive Church schools. Parishes should have the confidence to recognize that the Church school is a significant part of the Church's mission in the parish and an unrivalled opportunity for positive encounter with the wider community. Some clergy still regrettably see the Church school as a drain on their time and energies. The great majority of clergy have some involvement as a governor or in leading worship in schools. Whilst this involvement is often of excellent quality and highly valued, there is not at present enough opportunity through organized training and continuing ministerial education to develop the necessary skills.

Planning and progress?

In many local authority areas, the support of the Churches for the LEA and their need for partnership has led to warm co-operation. There seems to be a lack of rivalry and an understanding of the distinctiveness of the Church school. The new code of practice on the relationship between schools and LEAs explicitly mentions the services provided by diocesan authorities not just for Church schools but, in a number of aspects, for other schools as well. The Teacher Training Agency, promoting the new Learning Programme for Serving Head Teachers, recognizes that Church authorities might be able to offer helpful support from their experience on values education for head teachers of non-Church schools.

The 1998 Act gives effect to the Government's commitment to reduction in class sizes at Key Stage 1. This is likely to have a considerable impact beyond the first few years on class sizes at Key Stage 2. The Government recognizes that the implementation of the strategy cannot be at the expense of parental preference at popular schools and has allowed a substantial sum of money for capital development of schools in relation to the class sizes initiative. In the case of voluntary aided schools, government grant will be paid on 100 per cent of the capital costs. In some cases, this will allow popular, oversubscribed Church schools to expand. In addition the Government has made a commitment that LEA reorganization plans should not overall reduce the provision of places at Church schools within the authority.

The demand for places at school will continue to rise to the end of the century and beyond, especially at secondary level where the Church of England is particularly poorly represented. It will perhaps be possible to build on the security and popularity of the Church's position in statutory education and fulfil at last the Durham Report's recommendation 36 about national planning for Church school provision.

> The 'spread' of church voluntary aided schools should so far as may be possible be more rationally distributed, both geographically and within the educational system. To achieve this end a greater degree of centralised co-ordination will be necessary.

The dioceses are theoretically in a position themselves to plan provision centrally. The 1944 and 1973 Education Acts (Section 86 and Section 2 respectively) made it possible for dioceses to claim the proceeds of sale of closed schools to enable provision to be made elsewhere, whether or not the board of education or of finance was the trustee of the school. When rolls were falling in the seventies and eighties and property values were rising, a number of diocesan boards of education were able to establish or build up significant trust funds for capital works in new or existing schools. Dioceses have been able to make their own decision about the use of such funds. Under the 1993 Act it was established that it was lawful to use the interest to fund diocesan advisory and support staff. In a number of dioceses these funds (under Section 554 of the consolidated Education Act 1996) have been used to pay the whole or part of governing bodies' 15 per cent expenditure on capital and maintenance costs.

Planning and service provision at diocesan level is, however, not easy and some dioceses find it easier than others. Certain dioceses appear to have run their Section 554 funds down or to rely on the interest to fund their advice and support services to schools. In a number of dioceses such services are only maintained by imposing service charges on the schools. Since 1993 LEAs have had the power to pay the governors' 15 per cent. This has allowed some governing bodies to divert devolved LMS funds into the payment of their 15 per cent cost of a desirable small improvement project.

The provision of new schools, or even of relocated schools, is not always possible where it is desirable. Some LEAs are willing to pay the promoter's 15 per cent contribution for a new school, securing 85 per cent grant from the Government and a new school thereby without affecting their credit approvals. The developers of new housing areas can also be expected to make a contribution as a matter of planning gain. Many dioceses find that large sums of money can be raised to extend local schools or amalgamate them on one site but that this generosity is highly parochial. In the 1990s, a by no means affluent parish in the Diocese of Blackburn raised approaching £40,000 to extend their new building and, over four years, another parish raised £70,000 towards the cost of a relocated school. There are many similar examples. Dioceses have raised substantial sums and not just in the past, although perhaps few as considerable as the response to the Bishop's Appeal in Blackburn Diocese in 1949 which raised £125,000, equivalent to £3.4 million at today's prices.

There is another possible route for making funds more widely available where they are needed for the provision of more Church schools. It has recently been remarked that, in a shire county in the south of England containing two dioceses, one of the dioceses had no difficulty funding its 15 per cent for a new Church school, from accumulated Section 554 trust funds, while the other found it impossible. This is an area of the historic resources of dioceses which there has been no attempt to research let alone equalize. Some dioceses have clearly been better served by the closure and sale of redundant schools than have others.

If there is to be the national planning recommended by the Durham Commission in 1970, especially if there is to be a real extension in the provision of Church of England secondary schools, some means might have to be found for sharing the historic education resources of dioceses according to need, much as has been done in relation to funds administered by the Church Commissioners.

A new commission?

The report of the Durham Commission, set up in 1967, was published in 1970 under the title *The Fourth R*. It said:

> Only one thing is completely clear: on the subject of Church schools the Church of England has never had one generally agreed policy. It certainly has none today (page 217).

It reported twenty-six years after the 1944 Act. The years since *The Fourth R* have been years of considerable change. The Church has not been setting the agenda for education. If RE and Church schools are stronger or potentially so now more than ever, it is not only through the work of the Church but through the initiative of Government, partly but not exclusively out of concern for the moral education of the nation's young people. It is right to consider at this stage whether the Church might be ready for another major review. Then the Church of England would be well placed to estimate the true strengths of the present position and, on that basis, to build to one of greater strength for the Gospel through the changes recently enacted and which will inevitably come in the next few years.

The National Society

A Christian Voice in Education

The National Society (Church of England) for Promoting Religious Education supports everyone involved in Christian education – teachers, school governors, students, parents, clergy, parish and diocesan education teams – with the resources of its RE centres, courses, conferences and archives.

Founded in 1811, the Society was chiefly responsible for setting up the nationwide network of Church schools in England and Wales, and still helps them with legal and administrative advice for headteachers and governors. It was also a pioneer in teacher education through the Church colleges. The Society now provides resources for those responsible for RE and worship in any school, lecturers and students in colleges, and clergy and lay people in parish education. It publishes a wide range of books and booklets and a resource magazine, *Together with Children*.

The National Society is a voluntary body which works in partnership with the Church of England General Synod Board of Education and the Division for Education of the Church of Wales. An Anglican society, it also operates ecumenically, and helps to promote inter-faith education and dialogue through its RE centres.

For further details of the Society or a copy of our current resources catalogue and how you can support the continuing work of the Society, please contact:

The National Society
Church House
Great Smith Street
London SW1P 3NZ

Telephone: 0171-222 1672
Fax: 0171-233 2592
Email: NS@natsoc.org.uk

Values for Church Schools

Peter Shepherd

'Values in Education' is a term currently in vogue and there is a ground swell of opinion to bring values to the forefront of the educational debate in all schools. This book asks whether there are distinctive values that Church schools should identify and adapt, or should they follow the agenda set by the secular world?

Peter Shepherd is Head of Canon Slade School in Bolton and also an Anglican priest.

£4.00   ISBN 0 901819 61 1